When I was a young girl before m[...]*, I always laughed a lot and found life very exciting. My mother told me that when I was about two years old she took me to the seaside, and in those days there was a machine called The Laughing Sailor. She took me to see it and when you put a penny in the slot the sailor would just laugh and laugh. Well, one time my mother put a penny in the machine and the penny got stuck, so the sailor just went on laughing. I stood and watched it for a long time, then I fell asleep on the pavement. I was so small it made me very tired. I think that's why I laugh a lot today.*

When I reached my teens I remember my mother having a lot of fits. She was an epileptic and it used to frighten me a lot. My father would try not to let me see her in that condition, but sometimes he couldn't hide it. At that age I always used to dream of a big white cotton ball chasing me down the road and trying to suffocate me. I had a lot of fear in my heart but tried to overcome it with a laughing spirit.

What I went through with my father caused me to have a very rocky marriage for many years, but when I was able to forgive myself I found it easier to forgive him.

I was eighteen years old when I fell pregnant with my twins. When I gave birth to them I was put in an unmarried mothers' home for about four months and then my mother decided to bring us home to stay with her and my father. I was with them for about four months and then Nick returned to England and asked me to marry him. I decided to give it a try. That was forty years ago. We have had forty good years together and I have never regretted one day. It took me years to forgive Nick for walking out on me and the kids, but at last I managed to put it all behind me thanks to God.

Rosemary Panayiotou

MY LIFE OF VISIONS

*To Joyce with all my Love
Rosemary*

MY LIFE OF VISIONS

Rosemary Panayiotou

ATHENA PRESS
LONDON

MY LIFE OF VISIONS
Copyright © Rosemary Panayiotou 2006

All Rights Reserved

No part of this book may be reproduced in any form
by photocopying or by any electronic or mechanical means,
including information storage and retrieval systems,
without permission in writing from both the copyright
owner and the publisher of this book.

ISBN 1 84401 645 5

First Published 2006 by
ATHENA PRESS
Queen's House, 2 Holly Road
Twickenham TW1 4EG
United Kingdom

Printed for Athena Press

Preface

THIS BOOK IS BASED on my true life story. For many years I was longing to share these visions I have experienced, but I kept them deep within my heart, trying to fight the urge to put pen to paper. I eventually built up the courage to write this book, feeling very afraid that people might mock me because it is not always easy for people to believe what they read. But what I have shared with you in this book is very far from a lie.

I grew up in a big family – my mother had seven children. She was a very strict woman but a good mother, and she instilled us with many good principles and manners. I have always honoured her. We had a hard life but we were never short of anything. Religion did not play a part in my upbringing, and yet God reached me somehow.

I hope you enjoy reading this book as much as I have enjoyed writing it.

Rosemary Panayiotou

Contents

The Beginning of Truth	11
A Change of Heart	14
One Step Ahead	18
Unexpected Moment	22
No Chance of Winning	26
A Deep Cry from the Heart	29
Times of Loneliness	33
A Lesson to Learn	36
The Experience of Truth	39
To See with Spiritual Eyes	42
Unforgettable Miracle	45
One Bad Experience	48
Experiencing Physical Healing	51
Happiness on the Faces of our Children	54

The Beginning of Truth

LET ME BEGIN WITH an introduction. Hello there, everybody! My name is Rosemary Panayiotou – I have a Greek surname but I am English by birth; my husband is a Greek Cypriot. Anyway, I would really love to share my life story with you all. I believe it will give courage and hope to some people in this world today, because this is not an easy world to live in nowadays.

From the age of seventeen, I lived in London – such a busy city. I worked in a bakery shop – I used to love the bakery trade, I don't know why. Anyway, across the road used to be a restaurant and the name of it was Rose's Restaurant – can you believe it? Anyway, my future husband worked there as a chef. I don't know if you believe it, but most of the chefs were Cypriots. As the months went on, we started dating and, within no time, I realised I was pregnant. I was living with my parents and my mother was an old-fashioned woman. She happened to be Jewish, but not a very religious person. Well, with me vomiting in the mornings, it didn't take her long to realise what was wrong with me, so she arranged for me to go into a home for pregnant girls. I wasn't seeing so much of Nick at that time (that was the father's name). At seven months, they told me it was twins and they were due one month before I was eighteen. Nick came to the hospital twice to see us and then my mother appeared and told me that Nick had left the country and gone to South Africa.

I was devastated. I was trying to recover from a breech

The Beginning of Truth

birth, so my mother decided to take us home to stay with her, despite her disapproval. After seven months, Nick decided to come back and that's when we got married and off to South Africa we went. We stayed there for three and a half years. We both worked there and I cried every day, I was so homesick. But in the time I was there, I had very strange dreams about heaven. One of my dreams was about a very big cat, just lying on the carpet and there were all these birds flying around him. He just lay there so peacefully and then I heard a voice, a beautiful voice, behind me, so gentle, telling me to let this one bird out of the cage, to open the door and set him free. So, when I did, my hands came together and he flew right into them, so gently – he was pure white. I thought at the time it was a sign of peace but my life still carried on with terrible problems.

My twins – both girls – were about four years old by then. Nick's youngest brother was staying in South Africa at the time and he decided to go to Cyprus for a holiday. I suggested that he took the twins with him to meet their grandparents, whom they had never seen. While I was thinking about it, I had another dream. I dreamed of all these little boats tied to each other in a line, going across the water. Each one was covered up. As I stood before them, I lifted the covers and there was a great big white bear standing in the water. He told me not to touch the boats, but to let them go across the sea. The next day, after my dream, my husband and I decided to let the twins go for a holiday with their uncle. It wasn't long after that they left for Cyprus.

After about three weeks, Nick's father asked if the kids could stay longer as they were enjoying themselves so much. Anyway, as the time went on, they attended school

The Beginning of Truth

there and before we knew it, two years had passed and I was pregnant with another child. I decided to go back to England as I was so homesick, and then something very strange happened to me one morning. I was on my way to work, waiting at the bus stop, and everything went so quiet – the street, the road – as if I was the only person alive. An old man, dressed all in white from head to toe, sat at the bus stop with me and asked why I was so unhappy. I told him I was so homesick and that my children had been away for two years. As he walked away, he smiled at me and told me, 'Don't worry, everything will be all right, you'll see.' I turned and he was gone. For many years, that never left my mind.

Well, Nick and I went back to England, invested in a fish and chip shop and worked very hard. In the meantime, my son was born with a tumour. We christened him in the hospital and the tumour disappeared. We decided to sell the shop, bring our kids back home and go back to South Africa, and that's what we did. My twins went to school and we bought a lovely house.

Sometimes, we all wonder what life is all about, don't we? Anyway, we went back into business and started a small food takeaway and we did very well. In the years ahead, we started a few shops, worked them and then sold them on. We went back to South Africa in the year 1973 and a few years later, my mother came to visit us and stayed for about six months. She came to South Africa about three times in all.

As the years went on, I was heading into a deep depression and tried to commit suicide three times, but someone always turned up and stopped me. Anyway, my home became a battlefield and I was the one to blame.

A Change of Heart

IN MAY 1980, SOMETHING very strange happened in my life. On this particular night, my husband had his case packed and was going to leave us. I was lying on my bed and I remember crying out, 'Please, God, if you are real and you are really there, please help me. I don't know what to do.' Now, before this very deep cry, for many months I had been taking about thirty tablets a day for many different things.

Anyway, getting back to that night. As I cried out, I felt something come right through me and, in a split second, I saw the Lord Jesus go through the ceiling. The feeling was as though someone, or something, had filled up the emptiness I had been experiencing for many years. It was like the last piece of the puzzle had been found and I felt complete. Not knowing what had happened to me, I went into the living room and tried to explain to my husband, but he just didn't want to know. He said he had had enough.

Well, as the days went by, there were such changes in my life that were noticed by my children and husband. I was actually glowing and I was experiencing such peace and joy and there was such love coming forth from me. There was a big desire in me to read the Bible and this changed the lives of my children and my husband for ever. The Bible became a frequent subject of conversation in my home. My children had a Bible each and my husband had one in Greek. Anyway, as the years passed, my family became very close.

At this time, my twins were about fourteen years old. The years passed and I started to attend church and I got so close to Jesus. In the years ahead, the Lord gave me visions. One was when I was in my business – we had a little supermarket on the corner, near to where we were staying. It was about three o'clock one Sunday afternoon and I was reading a book behind the kiosk. I was the only one there as my husband was at home having a sleep. All of a sudden, the quietness took my attention. There were no cars going by and no customers in the shop. I knew the time, as we had a big clock at the other end of the shop. I then felt as if something very beautiful had surrounded the counter, but I didn't see anything. Then the Lord appeared right in front of me and He said to me, 'Do you understand, you belong to Me now? You are all Mine.' His fists were pounding on His chest and He was smiling. His eyes were shining so beautifully. Every muscle in my body went weak and I felt so full of joy. Then He went back and disappeared and whatever was surrounding the kiosk, followed Him.

At about five o'clock, my husband came back and when he tried to come near me he said, 'What's happened? You have a light all around you. It's as if you are glowing.' Well, that was a day I will never forget. If someone had told me years ago that these things were possible, I would have said they were crazy. I never realised that a man, who died two thousand years ago, could change my life today. Well, it's true, because He is *God*.

Anyway, let's get back to my life. A few years after I discovered Jesus, we sold the shop and then decided to sell the house and move to Cyprus for good. The twins were about twenty years old and my son about thirteen.

So, off we went. We sent on all our furniture and left for good – or so we thought. Well, have you ever sold up everything, gone overseas and then found out you didn't like it and wanted to go back? Yes, that's what happened to me. We stayed in Cyprus for three months and then went back to South Africa. We rented a house and found a big supermarket to buy. After nine months, we sold it to the wrong people and lost all the money we had worked for over the years – it was a big mistake. But while we were negotiating with the buyers one morning, we got up to go to the shop and discovered our twins had left home that night. My son didn't know anything. We were devastated. For many months we didn't know where they were. They were twenty-one years old then. Anyway, we hired private detectives and they found them living in a flat in Johannesburg, but as they didn't want to come home, we couldn't do anything.

In the meantime, the shop was sold but, overnight, the buyers sold the stock and left, so we lost all our money and were left with hardly anything. During this time, my husband developed diabetes. We decided to move to another area and try to start again, which we did but with a lot of debt. We carried on working for another seven years to try and improve the shop we bought. It was like having a bag with a hole in the bottom. We just couldn't get any further ahead, do you know what I mean? I think you do.

One of the twins never got in touch with us, but the other one phoned us two or three times, came back home for a couple of months then left again. We just couldn't please them. Anyway, we had the shop for seven years and then sold it to a Greek man who had no experience of business whatsoever. Well, he took over but he kept calling us back in to help him with different things. He gave us a deposit for the shop and payments every month for the balance. After about nine months, he slowly pulled out and left us with the shop again. In the meantime, we didn't know he was running up an overdraft with the bank and after another six months, the sheriff came and closed the shop. He put a lock on the door and we lost the rest of our money. It was a few hundred thousand and we had nothing to live on, so we decided to leave and go to Cyprus for good. Nick had a couple of very small pieces of land there, so we thought we would go and sell it and start again.

So, we were only in South Africa for about seven years, and we started to pack our few goods and sold our large pieces of furniture to the auctioneers, who gave us just a few pennies. The week before we left, we were asleep one night when four people broke into our home and stole our hi-fi, my silverware and a few more things. We really knew it was time to leave for good. What would you say?

So, my husband, my son (who was about twenty years old then) and I went to Cyprus and had to stay with Nick's father in the village. Well, have you seen some of the houses in the villages of Cyprus? The beds we laid on must have been running alive with lice and fleas. The toilet, in the yard, was a hole in the ground and there were spiders everywhere. The shower was a hosepipe over the grapevine in the yard and it was so dirty, I wanted to vomit all day. I couldn't eat anything. I had to do the washing in a big old bath in the yard and all our clothes were turning grey. I had left all the luxuries in South Africa. I felt like running away and never coming back. Nick's father was a wonderful old man and so full of love, but I know that if I hadn't known Jesus, I would never have made it. God was wonderful.

One Step Ahead

IT WAS JULY 1992 AND we had now been in Cyprus for a couple of weeks. We had lived in South Africa for twenty-six years and I was missing it so much. Anyway, we were sitting in a restaurant in a place called Latchi in Cyprus and the Lord spoke to me. God speaks to His people, you know. Anyway, He said to me, 'Do you see that man with no hair sitting over there?'

I said, 'Yes, Lord.'

He said, 'Tell Nick to go over to him. He is going to sell Nick's piece of land in the village.'

So I told Nick and he said, 'But Rose, I don't know him.'

So I said, 'I know, but Jesus does.'

So he said, 'OK, let's go.'

Anyway, we went to speak to the stranger and introduced ourselves and he told us that he was a lawyer who sold land part-time. Nick told him about the piece in the village and that we wanted to sell it. He told us that he knew a couple from Nicosia who were looking for a piece of land in the village. Well, a few days later, the lawyer came to the village with this couple. The husband was Scottish and the wife a Cypriot and they liked it immediately. We came to an agreement with the price at £23,000 and they accepted, but with a deposit of £8,000 and the rest over nine months. So, we had sold the land.

In the meantime, my husband found a job as a chef in the restaurant down the road towards the village. After a couple of weeks, one of Nick's cousins, who had a small leather shop across the road from where Nick was working, asked me if I would work it for him. I agreed and for seven months, Nick and I had jobs. I got the job in September 1992 and the following month, October, we found a small flat about two miles up the road. Slowly, everything was coming together. When Nick showed me the flat, I thought anything would do just to get out of the village, as I was working in the shop every day. I was keeping in touch with my kids in South Africa by phone. We decided to move into the flat. I thought, At last, my own place! Ladies, do you know what I mean? Anyway, we kept our jobs. The flat was partly furnished but had no washing machine. I thanked God for the bath; I would do my washing there. As the months passed, I felt a little bit better being on our own but I was missing my kids and South Africa so very much.

Well, returning to our move from South Africa to come to Cyprus. A few days before we left, I managed to trace my daughters and told them we were leaving and would love to see them before we went. They decided to come and see us one evening, and came to the house. My heart was broken when they told us that Michelle, one of the twins, had cancer and was having chemotherapy and the other twin had had a baby twelve months before and that the father was black. We both nearly collapsed – the shock was too much. Michelle had cancer of the bones and they had removed her ribs and no one had even notified us. Also, we didn't know that she had got married eighteen months before. Nick and I were devastated. Anyway, we sat down together and talked for a couple of hours. It was lovely to all be together again. We told them that we were going to Cyprus to live and that we would keep in touch, and we kept our word.

When we were in Cyprus, the twins were phoning me regularly but Michelle was getting worse – she was very, very ill. Christmas passed and April came, then May and Michelle was very bad and wanted to come over to us. We decided to send her the fare and she arrived in Cyprus on 16 June 1993. We collected her from Larnaca airport and she was in a wheelchair with oxygen and on her own. Mine and Nick's hearts were breaking. We laid her in the back of the car. She was very weak and we took her straight home. Nick and I stopped our jobs to be with her. We took her to the beach and out for supper a few nights, but every day she would just lie there and we could see she was getting worse. After five days, she had to go to hospital and was transferred from Paphos to Nicosia. We stayed with her all day and all night and she died on 25 June 1993. She was only twenty-seven years old. She had never smoked in her life and was like a model – a very beautiful girl. Her husband and my son came over from South Africa. Her twin sister, Donna, took it very badly and suffered mentally a lot. We buried her in the village where Nick, her father, was born. At the funeral, I sensed such strength from above – I can't put it into words.

As the days and months passed, I knew that life had to go on. It's not easy to lose a child and face life again. My heart goes out to all those people out there who have lost a child. I know how you are hurting. Please give Jesus a chance to help you. He loves you.

As the months passed, we had to start working again, so we decided to open a butchery in Paphos and found a lovely shop on the main street. So, about a year after Michelle died, we opened up. We were doing so well; we

One Step Ahead

employed a butcher from England to help us and a Cypriot girl to clean. We were very busy. I put one van out on the road delivering and was ready to put out another one. This was all within one year of opening. By then, my daughter had been dead for two years.

Suddenly, one Saturday morning in October 1995, we had a phone call from South Africa. Nick's youngest brother had been shot seven times and had died the day before. We were so shocked and Nick's father was taken very ill with the shock. But God was still faithful and gave us strength. On Saturday 9 December at 10 p.m. we decided to take a ride to the shop and check the fridges were working OK. It took about forty-five minutes from where we lived and, on the way back, about five minutes from home, the most tragic thing happened—

Before I tell you, I would like to say that life is so unpredictable. None of us know what will happen in the next five minutes. That's why it is so important to enjoy life to its fullest. I believe, and have always believed, that to laugh is the best form of medication you can have…

Unexpected Moment

SO, WE WERE JUST FIVE minutes from home on our way back from the shop. The roads had a lot of bends and I remember my husband saying, 'Oh my God!' and I was aware of the speed of this oncoming car, not seeing anything at the time because of the bend. My husband pulled to the side and slowed right down. There were mountains on both sides. Then, this Mercedes turned the bend and lost control. The next thing I remember was saying to my husband, 'Nick, he's hit us!' I said it three times and then I must have lost consciousness.

I very vaguely remember the doctor leaning over me and saying, 'Rosemary, we must check your brain,' and I can remember going into a tunnel.

Well, when I woke two days later, I had an iron frame on my face and a patch over my left eye. I was hurting all over. A few hours later, the doctor came and laid his hand on my shoulder. I was in a room with thirty other patients and there were cockroaches in my side cabinet. The doctor said, 'Rosemary, you have lost your left eye.' At the time I thought, Well, that's not so bad. It didn't hit me – I didn't realise the mental effect it would have on me later in life. I asked the sister where my husband was. She said he was upstairs and he was fine. I asked her if he was alive and she said yes, he was OK. When I laid in bed, I looked around the ward but I had to hold my right eye open as it was so bruised.

Well, the next day, I decided to get out of bed and

have a shower, not even thinking, Are my legs OK? Thank God the rest of my body was just terribly bruised.

In the meantime, my son came over from South Africa to carry on the business with the couple of staff we had working there, and my sister and brother came over from England to see us. When my son came to the hospital, I saw him crying at the door and I called him over. I said to him, 'Andrew, don't worry about anything. Everything is going to be all right. You go back to the shop and look after the customers and Daddy and I are going to be fine.'

My son was only twenty-three years old, but somehow I knew all was going to be well.

I asked my sister to shower me as I felt so dirty. When I looked into the mirror, I couldn't believe what I saw. My head was swollen to twice its original size; my face was cut to pieces and badly bruised. I had stitches all over. I looked at myself and said, 'My God, my face, I can never hide the damage!' I had never felt so ugly in my whole life. I was about forty-seven years old; life was just starting to begin for me; my children were off hands and my husband and I were looking forward to the years ahead, and to enjoying them together.

Well, during the next two to three years, I had ten operations – four on my eyes and six on my face. The left eye was severely damaged and I lost the socket, my eyelid and part of the bone above the eye, as well as the eye itself.

My right eye had fallen at the back and sunk a little and my nose had been hanging off. I ended up with steel plates with eight screws on the right side of my face, from my nose to the side of my face. I lost the nerve above my right lip and I had no sense of smell or taste. I

Unexpected Moment

was left with a big scar right across my face. Well, as the years went on, my face started to take shape and form. The Lord was so good to me. I had my eye operations in Moorfields Hospital, London.

My husband's injuries were very severe. When the car hit us, Nick's hipbone was on the seat and his leg was broken in five places. His lung was pouring blood. He was a diabetic – how he survived, only God knows. He was left with a short leg and his right foot turns inwards. The bone of his hip sticks out, like a ball, and he is very uncomfortable but every day we thank God for His mercy and grace. That's why we love Him so much. Just after the accident, Nick had gangrene right down his right leg but the doctors saved it, so, we have a lot to be grateful for.

A year after the accident we decided to move our butchery into a supermarket. The owner had asked us to move our equipment into his shop. When we thought about it, we thought it would be easier to manage – it was a smaller area. So, we signed a five-year contract.

Six months after the accident, my son went back to South Africa and had lost a lot of study time at university. At the time, I felt that the whole world was against us; we didn't know which way to turn. Anyway, we moved into the supermarket and managed with the staff we had. At the time, I was going back and forth to England for treatment.

Well, one year after we moved into the supermarket, Nick's father died. He was eighty-four years old. I loved him very much. He couldn't speak English, but somehow we understood each other, though I don't know how because my Greek was like double Dutch! Remember, my friends, what I said earlier – the best medicine is smiling and laughing. It will bring you through anything, even though it's not always easy to do. I call you friends because you are my friends, that's why I want to share my life with you.

Well, when we lost Nick's dad, life still had to go on. As the months passed, the butchery wasn't very busy. Trade had gone down in the supermarket, so we started to get behind with certain payments and life was very hard. For me to go to England for treatment, we were borrowing money and getting into debt to survive.

No Chance of Winning

A YEAR AFTER NICK'S father died, I had a call from England to say my mother had passed away. Everything seemed so hard to bear, but life still had to go on. Thank God for Jesus and His love and support. Mother died on 30 July 1998. She was my best friend – the only one on earth who really wanted the best for us.

Well, it was about three years since we had moved our butchery into the supermarket and we had regretted it every day since we'd made the move. About four months later I woke up one morning with a very strange feeling inside me. I said to Nick, 'I believe God is taking us out of this shop very soon. We are coming out.' Within two months, we heard that the owner had sold the supermarket to a very big company and we were going to be told to leave; they didn't want a butchery in there. The date was 20 April 1999. The owner of the supermarket sent us a lawyer's letter to instruct us to be out by the end of that month – he gave us about seven days. We had no place to put our equipment and no other shop to go to, so our living was completely cut off. The man had sold his supermarket, got a few million and left us with nothing.

So, on 27 April, we left our equipment there and the new owner offered us £3,000 for the lot. It was worth about £20,000 but we had no choice but to accept.

By this time I was so fed up, and we didn't know what to do. Nick's case in the court was still going through and mine hadn't even started. It was nearly five years since the accident. We owed the bank so much money and owed money to certain private people. I kept thinking, Why is this happening to us? I was still on a lot of medication because of the accident and the medical insurance would not cover an ongoing illness, so it was costing us a lot of money every month to buy medication for the pain. Sometimes, life can be so hard. I would look at other people and just see them sail through life so easily. I used to think we must be such sinners but, as time went on, I thought, Well, it's got to get better.

At the beginning of the year 2000, my case went to court. The lawyer phoned me two weeks before and asked me to go and see him in his office so that we could go through the case. I hadn't heard from him for over a year. Anyway, I went there and he questioned me on a few things and told me that they would cross-examine me on the stand. I had never stood in court before for this type of thing, so you can imagine how nervous I was – especially in a strange country and not understanding the language.

Well, the day came and I took the stand. The judge looked very cold and hard. In Cyprus, women don't mean very much – they are always held down. I was shaking. Anyway, the case went on for two and a half hours, then there was a thirty-minute break and then another two hours without a chair or a glass of water to drink. A few months previously, I had undergone a treatment for my eyes. I was very weak and nearly collapsed on the stand but was too afraid to say anything. I felt like a criminal and not the victim.

Let me go back a little and tell you about the people in the car that hit us. There were two men, in their late thirties. The driver died instantly – his neck broke. The passenger died six hours later from internal bleeding. We were told that they were headmasters of a local school. When they hit us, their speedometer showed one hundred and fifty kilometres. How we survived, God only knows.

Back to my court case: they put me on the stand three times. The second time, I was on the stand for three hours and the third time for three and a half hours. I was so exhausted by the time it had finished. My doctor from Moorfields in England would not come over for the court hearing and the lawyer told me that it would make my case very weak. I would say to my lawyer, 'But the court has the doctor's reports,' and he would shout and say, 'I told you, they mean nothing in the court. We might as well throw them in the dustbin! The doctor should be there personally.'

I asked my lawyer who would pay for the hotel while he was here and he told me that I must. I told him I couldn't and he told me to sort it out.

Anyway, my case finished on 6 July 2001, but the doctors from England never turned up to testify. The lawyer never even fought in court for the loss of business for us. You see, over here there is not much choice with lawyers and they are not that advanced, so you just put up with what you can get. If our accident had happened in America or England, we would have been much better off, but that's life. Deep down inside of me, I knew my Lord Jesus wouldn't let me down, somehow I knew He would help me.

A Deep Cry from the Heart

WELL, WHEN MY case had finished in court, we had opened another shop in the February of that same year. My brother, who had been living over here for eight months before February, moved here permanently with his third wife and her seventeen-year-old daughter. We got him the small flat next to us, to rent. He painted it up and made it comfortable, so we decided to open the butchery together because Nick couldn't do the things he used to because of his injuries. We thought it would be a great help and we could build the business up and try to get outside orders by the time my brother had learned the trade. Well, the first few months were not too bad and by the time my case had finished in July, my brother went to renew his papers to stay in Cyprus. He had no money in the bank so they refused him another year and they told him he had to go back. Now, my brother, John, had already invested in the shop about £18,500 but, by that time, we owed the suppliers about £7,500 and still needed stock.

Well, my case in court finished on 6 July. Nick got his money for the accident on 16 July and John went back to England on 24 July. When Nick got his money, the bank took three-quarters of it and with the rest, we had to pay for all the equipment and pay the suppliers. To put stock in the business, we had to take an overdraft. Now, altogether, Nick and I had invested about £40,000 in the business so we thought the best thing to do was to keep the shop going. We had a lady for cleaning but she left and Nick and I were on our own. Truly, I tell you, if it wasn't for the Lord, I think I would have bought a gun and just blown my life right away.

John went back to England with hate in his heart. He blamed us for everything and never wanted to talk to us again. He and his wife were sending us threatening letters and making cold and bitter phone calls. They wanted their money back and we didn't have any. The business was still new and we worked like a couple of dogs, with no wages to this day, just covering our expenses.

John went back in July 2001 and it is now November 2002, and I am still waiting to hear the result of my case from the judge. They have no juries in the courts in Cyprus so the judge decides the final amount. My husband and I are still working the shop today. He is sixty-three and I am fifty-four. We invested so much money and still owe the bank plenty.

Sometimes in our lives, we make the wrong moves and decisions and we pay so dearly. It's funny – we don't feel sorry for ourselves, we try to enjoy every day because life is so precious and in the end, so rewarding if we know Christ as our personal saviour. You know, I really believe the words we spoke years ago influence our lives today. I believe our words are very powerful; they bless or curse us. How careful we must be!

I would like to share a very strange experience that happened to me when we first moved to South Africa. It was in the year 1968 in the September, the first day we arrived there. We went to stay with Nick's brother, the eldest brother, and his wife and three children. Well, the day we arrived, Nick's sister-in-law had arranged a lovely dinner party at the house and had invited about fifty people to come. Now, I had never met any of them before, so I felt very nervous. Anyway, on that evening, I was sitting in the chair and feeling very strange. As I looked around the room, I started to realise that I had been in that room before. I started to remember the chairs, the curtains and the carpets. I felt very afraid and called my husband over and told him. He thought it was very strange. I said to him, 'Nick, I know who is going to come through the door next.' So I described the people, a husband and wife, what colour clothes they had on, the colour of their hair and what they were going to say. As we both turned around, it happened exactly as I had predicted. My husband went white, as if he had seen a ghost. I could never explain it as I had never been out of England in my whole life – well, I am sure many of you out there must have had similar experiences. Don't you think life is so unpredictable? There are many things that we go through that we can't explain but that we never forget.

I would like to tell you about something else that happened to me. It was in the year 1985 but I can't remember the month. Well, that's irrelevant. Anyway, four of us had gone out to the Holiday Inn for a meal. There was my husband and I, and another couple. We had ordered our supper and were sitting there having a good laugh. The waiter had just put my supper in front of me when I had something strange happen. It was like a flash, right in front of me. I saw a man walk into a bedroom where two children were sleeping. One was about five years old and the other about two. He put a gun to both of their heads and shot them in cold blood. I didn't understand why I saw this or what it was all about, but as I heard the shots,

I jumped and was so sad that night that I didn't sleep very well.

The next morning, I got up and dressed to go to my business and I picked up the newspaper on the way. Right on the front page was an article about a father of two who had been suffering deep depression and had shot his two kids and then himself at twelve o'clock the night before. Now, I had the vision at about seven o'clock that night. Sometimes, when I think back, maybe it was to tell me to pray, but I didn't understand at the time why I saw this, but I have never forgotten. It was like a warning sign to always pray for others and God will take care of us. Sometimes, my heart cries many tears when I think of the world we live in.

Times of Loneliness

THERE'S SO MUCH PAIN AND suffering out there. If we could all say a small prayer every day for others, I believe it could make a difference. It's funny but I have always had a soft spot for those who are in prison and more so for those on death row. My heart breaks for them because in a way, sometimes in every one of our lives we feel like a prisoner one way or the other. I know I did when I lost my daughter to cancer. I felt I had been closed in. I felt nobody understood the hurt and pain I felt. I wish I had died with her, and it's only if you go through this type of thing you can understand others when they lose a child. I can feel their pain and suffering. My mind goes back many times to when I was only seventeen and was pregnant with the twins. I think of how lost and lonely I felt. I remember a very distinct time when I was about three months pregnant and I was walking home from work. I was living with my parents then and, as I was walking home, the street was very quiet and it was quite a dark night. I was so troubled in my heart and mind and I was thinking of so many things. I then heard a very quiet and beautiful voice call my name, telling me not to worry, everything was going to be all right. I thought someone was behind me, so I looked round quickly but the street was empty, no one was to be seen. I thought I was going mad, but I know I heard it.

I remember once when I was about six months pregnant, I was still living with my parents. Nick and I went out and he took me to the casino in Streatham. While he was playing blackjack, Nick kept passing all his loose silver to me and I was putting it in my pocket. That night I got home late and my mother was waiting up for me and was very mad. I told her where we had been and she threw me out. I was seventeen and six months pregnant, so I got a taxi to Nick. Luckily, I had all the silver he had given me that night, otherwise I would have had to walk. Well, I stayed with him for a few days and then went into an unmarried mothers' home.

There was a time in my life when my mother and father sent me for the weekend to a couple who were doing abortions in their home. I didn't know what was going on until I got there and I was so afraid. Well, they tried every way to bring my babies down but it just didn't happen. I always believe it wasn't meant to be. So, if there are any unmarried mothers out there today, remember God loves you and He has a plan for you. Look to Him and He will bring you through it all. If you don't know what decision to make, ask God to help you and show you what to do, because it is very hard when you are going through it on your own; the world can be a very lonely place. Don't ever be afraid to call on Jesus, He is always there. It's funny – I speak a lot about the Lord God Almighty and yet I am not a religious person at all, but I know from experience what God can do for you. What He has done for me, He can do for you, just give Him a chance. I didn't mean for this to be a religious book, so don't put it down yet.

We went to South Africa for the first time in 1968, and the following year I found work as a cashier in a big supermarket. I was finding it very hard because a lot of

Afrikaans was spoken then and I wasn't a person who could pick up languages very well, so I battled with the customers a lot. Anyway, it was a very good experience for me and I suppose it helped me to grow up a little.

One day, when I went to work, I walked in and straight away I realised something was going on. They had about fifty staff working there and about every ten minutes, someone was called to the office and given an envelope, then they walked out of the door. My heart was pounding inside me. I thought they were going to fire me too. I didn't know what was going on but, one by one, all the staff were leaving. I was the last one to be called up and I was so frightened. There were about six big bosses in the office and they told me to sit down. They said to me that they wanted me to work in the office to do the wages and the books. Well, I was never very clever at school and never went to college, but they said they would train me. I said all right, but why has everybody left? They told me everybody had been pinching money from the business, so they were going to employ new staff. I was the only one they kept out of all the fifty staff. I was quite honoured. Anyway, they trained me and I really did enjoy my work. The manager was Afrikaans and always reminded me of a sergeant major in the army. Well, I didn't let that worry me too much.

A Lesson to Learn

WHEN WE WENT BACK to South Africa in 1973, I realised I loved that country so much and I didn't want to live anywhere else in the world, as I mentioned earlier. In the year 1977, my mother came over to stay with us for a holiday. She had never been out of England before. It was a wonderful experience for her and it was so lovely to have her with us. She was like my best friend. She stayed with us for six months, as I said. She loved it and we enjoyed every moment with her. Since she has died, I look back and cherish those times we had with her. She was always a happy, cheerful person and nice to be around.

There was a time in my life when my mother was in hospital having my younger sister, and the other six of us were at home with Dad. Well, at that time I was about ten years old and none of us, including Dad, really worried about cleaning the house while Mum was away. Anyway, when she was due to come home, we all had to give it a good spring clean, as Dad said. My father was an old soft spot and we all took liberties with him. He came upstairs and told me to clean my bedroom and I just sat there. He had never hit any of us. Well, I started to push my luck. I said to him, 'No, I don't feel like it,' and he asked me again. He said, 'Your mother's coming home tomorrow.'

Well, I couldn't care less, so he gave me one slap round the face. I couldn't believe what he'd done. I got

A Lesson to Learn

up quickly and my room was shining in less than an hour. Sometimes, we need a little push. What do you say, ladies?

Anyway, as I was growing up, we used to do a lot of camping at weekends with our parents. We had some good times. My mother took everything with us – it was like a home from home. My brother and I used to do a lot of fishing but I was always the one to take the fish off the hook. My brother didn't like the sight of blood – he wasn't very brave, but I loved him very much. He had lovely blond curly hair. I remember many times, the wind was blowing and my father tried to put a tent up. It was a blow-up type and we used to have so many laughs. I bet you all have some stories to tell about growing up.

There was a time when I was about thirteen, I went to the park with my friends and got my head stuck in the bars and people were trying to push me from both ends to get me out. At last the police came and got me out and took me home in their car. When I got in, I got a hiding on top of everything for coming home in a police car. All the neighbours saw me and in those days, people used to worry about what other people said.

When I was about thirteen, my mother bought a caravan. My father was fed up with the tent. I don't blame him, do you? Well, we had some good times every weekend at the seaside. Now, many times I sit thinking about the things my kids got up to when they were small and would give anything to have those times back again. I try to correct the wrongs I did, bringing my kids up. There's so much I would like to make right, but we can't turn the clock back. So, I speak to all you young mothers out there – I know, as a mother, you are trying your best, but give the kids as much love as you can. It's the love that will always keep them close to you, even when they are older. Give them plenty of love and understanding and you will never lose them.

Many times I think of my childhood and the times when my life was in danger and the Lord always saved me. At the time, I didn't know it was the Lord but when I think back, it all seems to fit like a puzzle.

Well, my husband and I have been living in Cyprus now for nearly eleven years and my two children live in South Africa in the meantime. My daughter has married the father of her son and she has just recently had another son. The father is a South African black man. My son is nearly thirty-one years old and is not married yet. He has been a wonderful, loving and well-behaved child, always keeping in contact with us and always concerned about our welfare. My husband always longed for a big family. Well, every day, we thank God for the children we have.

Coming up to my next chapter, I want so much to share with you some wonderful dreams and visions I had in the past, but please, I want you to keep an open mind and try not to be sceptical about what you are going to read. Everything that I am going to share with you will be the truth, the whole truth and nothing but the truth. I can't blame anyone who reads this and doesn't believe it because I think if I didn't know Jesus as a personal friend, maybe it would be hard for me to believe what I am about to share with you. All I ask is that you understand that anything today is possible. Most of us know that strange things are happening these days.

The Experience of Truth

PLEASE REMEMBER ONE thing before I start – I am not a religious person. I do believe that Jesus Christ was not a religious man. He is our Maker and I believe He longs for fellowship with us and He wants only the best for us. What a wonderful thing to know – the Creator wants to talk with His creation. Sometimes, it's not easy to talk to someone you can't see, but believe me, He hears everything you say and, if it comes from your heart, you will receive an answer. I have shared a few experiences of dreams and visions with you, so now I would like to share the rest. I know it won't be easy for you to believe, but please keep an open mind. You don't know what God has got in store for you in the future. All I know is, He loves you very much.

Well, let me get started. The experience I had with Jesus Christ was in 1980. Believe me, I was one of the biggest swearers in the country. I mean, really bad words used to come out of my mouth. I came from a home that used bad language and for many years, I had used bad words regularly, every day.

Well, the Lord came into my life in 1980. A few months had passed and, in those days, I was working in our business. It was a small supermarket on the corner. On this particular day, I was serving at the counter and all of these boys came in – about twenty of them all together – and they wouldn't wait, they all wanted to be served at once. I felt myself getting very angry with all of them and I started to use the bad language I had been using for years. As I spoke these words, I had never felt so disgusted with myself. I asked my husband to take over and I remember going to the back of the shop in the storeroom. I fell to my knees and started to cry and then I looked slightly to my side and I saw someone with a pair of sandals on and a very long white cloak come in the door. I felt two hands very gently placed on top of my head and this gentle voice told me to go back to my work, I had been forgiven. At that very moment, I felt clean again. Please understand, it is not easy to put these experiences into words, but I am describing it exactly as it happened. I knew I had been forgiven and so I could go about my work as before.

Not very long after that, there was another time in my life when one of my customers was dying of cancer. I didn't know, but I could see she was getting very nasty and angry all the time. Then, a few weeks passed and I didn't see her and I wondered if she was all right. Anyway, one afternoon I needed to go home and have a lie down. I was sort of half asleep and half awake when I heard this soft voice tell me three times to go and read my Bible at the side of Mrs Jacobs. It was winter outside and it felt very cold so I thought I would go later. I didn't get there that day. Now, somehow, deep within me, I knew it was that lady. I never, ever knew her name but when the Lord told me, somehow inside me, I knew it was her.

The next morning, I went to the shop thinking I would go today. As I entered the shop at about eight o'clock, someone put their hand on my shoulder and said to me, 'Rose, did you know Mrs Jacobs died last night at about twelve o'clock?' I felt my whole inside drop to the

The Experience of Truth

floor. I never reached her in time to tell her about the Lord. Thank God He forgives us so many times. That was a lesson I learned over the years – to listen when God speaks.

Anyway, about a year passed and something else happened to me. It was about two o'clock in the early hours of the morning. I got up to go to the bathroom and, as I opened my eyes, there was this very powerful and beautiful presence all around my bed. It felt like a presence of love and peace and seemed to take my breath away. As I walked to the bathroom, it came with me and then came back round the bed. Well, when I woke in the morning, I could hardly speak and when I did, the only words that came out of my mouth were, 'Truly, He is the Son of God.' That was all I could say for about six hours and, in that time, there was a light around my body.

Now, these things were all new to my husband and me. I never knew things like this happened to people. After I found Jesus, I used to pray maybe about five hours a day. Every chance I had, I would be on my knees. I wanted to know Him so much. I was going to church five nights a week – I couldn't get enough.

Now, readers, please remember all this happened many years before the car accident, so we can't say my brain had been shaken. What I am sharing with you is the whole truth and I really needed to write this book. For many years I have been carrying these experiences inside me. I felt someone out there might need to hear about all this. It might be an encouragement to someone.

To See with Spiritual Eyes

WHEN I LIVED IN SOUTH Africa for all those years, we owned many supermarkets. We had a supermarket in an area called Bedford View. It was a lovely area and a very rich place. There were about fourteen shops in the same complex and there were offices, too. Well, most of the people that worked there used to come and buy at our shop. On this particular day, I was working on one of the tills and there were about ten people waiting to be served. One of the chaps in the queue used to work in the offices. I had served him a few times before I noticed that he had a sort of lump on his back and he was kind of bent over a bit, but I never used to take much notice of this. Now, please don't take what I am going to tell you wrongly; it was something that was shown to me by God. I could never have seen this with my own eyes and I am not saying that people who have bent backs might have a demon. Anyway, when he got to me to be served, I saw a small type of monkey on his shoulder. It kept hiding behind his head and looking straight at me. It was so ugly – I couldn't believe what I was seeing. I had never seen anything like this in my whole life. The only thing I kept thinking was, It is so ugly, what is it? Now, no one else could see it. After I served him and he had left, I sat there so shocked my husband asked me what was wrong. I told him. I don't know if he believed me but when he looked at me, he knew I had seen something, as I was completely white and shocked.

Many times I sit and think about all these things, but when I read the Bible, I know it's not unusual to see what I've seen because Jesus saw these things too. I believe many of you out there have had different experiences in your life and probably have never shared them with anyone just in case they think you are going mad. Well, I don't, because many things are happening these days that we have no explanation for. So remember, you are not alone. If you look it up in the Bible, you will see things like yours and mine happened thousands of years ago. So remember, God's watching you and He loves you.

Now, I never came from a home where any of us ever saw into the supernatural world, but I do believe that God, in these last days, is showing dreams and visions to many people. He is trying to speak to us all in different ways and trying to warn us that He is coming back. He came before, why shouldn't He come again? He said He would. All my life while I was growing up, as a family we never held a conversation about God, and yet my mother was a God-fearing woman, but not my father. I don't think he ever believed in anything. Well, he never told any of us if he did. My father died in 1972. He was a man you could sit and talk to about anything. He was very soft and understanding. I believe we should try and see the good in everybody if we can. God put good in us all but sometimes, the evil seems to overpower the good and doesn't give it a chance to come to light. I love people – any colour, any nationality – because everybody has got something to share and a story to tell.

It's funny how we all believe our own culture and nationality is the best. When I first married my husband, it was so difficult for me to understand his ways. The

Cypriots are very different to the English. They are brought up to have so much control over their wives and children – it took me years to understand him. I really believe that if it hadn't been for Jesus, we would probably not be together today. I am not saying I was easy to live with. I really believe I was one of the most difficult people to live with. I wanted it all my own way. Now, that's something you just don't get living with a Greek, especially if you're a woman. Well, we can say today that we are one of the happiest couples on earth, thanks to the Lord.

When I had my twins, I was very young and mixed up. I had no idea how to handle my children – I was just a child myself. I came from a home where there was not a lot of love shown. My mother had seven kids and she was an epileptic, so it was very hard for her. As we grew up, we never learned how to show love, so naturally my kids suffered too. I had a lot of hate and jealousy in my heart that reared its nasty head every now and then; that's what turned my home into a battlefield. I wanted so much to show love and bring my kids up the right way but I didn't know how. You see, the good is in us but we don't know how to let it come forth. Well, that's where Jesus comes in. He shows us how to love with His love. The beautiful thing is, we don't have to try because He will love people through you, if we let Him.

Unforgettable Miracle

I REMEMBER WHEN WE were kids, at the beginning of the year we would promise ourselves we would make a New Year's resolution, we would try to do something good this year. Well, before I'd reached two months I couldn't keep it up and I would give in, but with Jesus it lasts because He does it through you, there is no effort. I love it, don't you? We don't have to try to be something we are not. Christ does it through us – I think that is why I feel for those in prison because that is how I felt for so many years: I felt caged in, I couldn't escape. Please don't misunderstand me; I am not saying we will be perfect or we will not do anything wrong, but I am saying it will be much easier to do good and it will last.

I want to share another miracle that happened to me about thirty-one years ago when my son was only about a year old. Well, the incident happened about then and the miracle itself took place in 1980. We were living in South Africa at the time. That was when we had our own little takeaway business. It was a beautiful, lovely, clean-looking shop with a lovely atmosphere, but we were working many hours and even seven days a week.

The shop had a lovely big backyard so my son could play at the back while we were working. We had about five staff working for us and it was a very busy little shop. I loved it. Well, this particular night we were on our way home. I was sitting in the front, my husband was driving and my son was on my lap. The staff were sitting in the back, as on every other night. I said to my husband, 'Nick, be careful.' I could see a car coming towards us; he was still very far away but he was going all over the road. By the time I had finished saying what I wanted to say he had hit us head on. We weren't going very fast, my door swung open and me and my baby were thrown onto a field. I didn't feel hurt, just a few bruises; I felt all right and my baby was fine and everybody else was OK. The car was a write-off.

Anyway, as the years went on, I didn't know my spine was deteriorating slowly as a result of the accident. Each cushion in between the spine, which the doctors call disks, was wearing away. In time – well, within about five to six years – I was left nearly paralysed. I could hardly walk and I was limited in what I could do. I went to a specialist and chiropractors and I was advised in the end to have an operation, although there was very little hope of my ever walking again. But, God had different plans. In the meantime I found Christ as my Saviour in May 1980 and in August the same year my back left me completely bed-ridden with pain. I had a small tape recorder so I decided to play some Christian tapes to raise my faith. On one of these tapes the preacher said, 'By His stripes ye were healed.' I couldn't understand what he meant so I kept playing it over and over again and then I thought if I was healed, that was past tense so why am I lying in this bed, sick and in pain? Something is wrong; God is not a liar so something is wrong.

Then the miracle came. I heard a voice telling me to get up and that there was nothing wrong with my back. It was the most beautiful voice I have ever heard. First of all I thought I was imagining it and then I heard it again. I got up and there was no pain at that moment. It was hard to believe; I couldn't stop crying. My daughter came in and told me to get back into bed. I told her what had happened, and she began to cry too. For years I had been unable to bend, so I tried to bend and I was afraid the pain might come back. I heard the voice again telling me not to be afraid and to bend as many times as I wanted to as there was nothing wrong with my back. I got dressed and went to the shop and told my husband the story. We all rejoiced.

I had X-rays done of my spine after this miracle and it was straight and the disks were all replaced. That was twenty-three years ago.

What I am sharing with you in this book, I have not shared with a lot of people before, but every word is true. Please read this book with an open mind. Remember, nothing is impossible to those who believe. My own children were witness to the miracles. If you asked me why these things have happened to me I can't answer you. Maybe, it's to write this book to let others know that Jesus lives and what He's done for me He will do for you, only believe. Many of you may ask, Why do so many people in the world suffer? Remember, the devil is wicked but God is love. I believe we are living in days when it is hard to make it on your own. This world seems to encourage people to get into debt. When you watch TV or go anywhere they advise loans or credit cards with such a low interest rate but then if you go over your repayment time the interest doubles then God help us all. We find it so hard to pay it back. You see the devil's system. A lot of people appear to get caught in the spider's web. This is one of the reasons Jesus came to set us free, not only from sin but also from Satan's system. Finally we can find freedom, if we want it.

One Bad Experience

BEFORE I KNEW THE Lord, I would suffer spells of very deep depression and I was always very lonely. I felt I had to be around a lot of people and then I was OK. I always appeared to other people as a very happy person but deep within I was crying for help and didn't know where to find it. I believe this world can be very lonely, even if you have a lot of friends, because the truth is we belong to God and inside we cry out for Him daily. The same way doctors say each of us has a little bit of cancer in our bodies, well, every one of us has a little piece of God in us too and we are trying to find the peace we want. Most of my visions were in the early years of my Christian walk. If someone asked me many years ago if I was a Christian, I would say yes, but inside I didn't even know what it meant. However, these days I am one hundred per cent sure that I am.

Now, this vision I want to share with you might be very hard for you to believe but please read this book with a very open mind, as I've requested before. Don't put it down yet; what I am sharing with you really did happen to me.

Anyway, many years back, my twins were about sixteen years old. It was 1982 and it was a Saturday afternoon at about four o'clock. We had a small supermarket up the road from our house. I decided to go home and have a swim in our pool. It was lovely and quiet in our back garden. I swam a little and then lay down on the grass on my stomach. I was all alone – well, I thought I was. I was just closing my eyes when I felt something blowing gently against my head and as I looked up I saw Jesus standing there. He was smiling and he told me to swim. He said he loves to see us happy in the water. I told him it was a bit cold and he just smiled and said, 'Please swim.' So, I did, up and down and he was standing on the side laughing with me. A little while after, I climbed out and was sat on the grass drying myself when my daughter, Michelle, came to the back gate and the Lord said, 'Look, look, there's another one of my children.' I asked Michelle to come because the Lord was calling to her but when I turned, He was gone. I asked my daughter if she had seen Him; she said she hadn't but she wished she had. I can never forget these times and moments; they were very special to me because they were real. In the book of John 14, Verse 21, He tells us if we keep His commandments He will manifest Himself to us. That means He will physically show Himself to us. How precious that is.

I really wanted to share this book with you all out there because it's funny, isn't it; when someone does good things for you we can't keep it to ourselves – we want to share it with someone! Even if someone hurts us we just want to tell everybody our side of the story but if we have been abused by a family member or anyone it's just something we keep to ourselves because we feel we are to blame and that it's our fault so we find we can't share. Now Jesus is the healer of something that hurts so deep. There is no one on earth who can help you to forgive someone who might have caused you so much pain. Now, I bet you are wondering why I am mentioning something like this. Well, it's not something you can

One Bad Experience

heal yourself or just push away as the years go on, and you cannot pretend it never happened. It's like a scar that never goes away unless it's treated with gentleness, understanding and love, only God's love.

I was a victim: as a child, I was sexually abused by my father. I was never able to share this with anyone, not even my own husband. I wasn't sure if he would understand the mental damage it did to me over the years. Well, knowing the Lord as my Saviour helped me to forgive my father many years ago and helped me deal with the guilt I was carrying.

My father died about thirty years ago and I can say today that I hold no hate towards him. I believe that in his own way he loved us kids very much. I don't believe his sin was any bigger than any of mine. We all sin in different ways. May God forgive us all.

This book is to help you understand that anything we go through in life and anything that goes against us we can still come through victorious if we know Jesus.

Well, at last I received my cheque from the court for my accident and I was able to clear all our debts at the banks and pay back everybody we owed money to. I thank God that I was able to buy a small home and some nice furniture.

Nick and I still have the butchery and the business is picking up and we have cut our hours down. At last we are living quite a good life. We will always live with the damage from the accident, but we pray and hope every day for the miracle of healing.

Experiencing Physical Healing

I BELIEVE GOD'S TIMING is always right. I want to share with you certain things about my operations due to the accident. The first operation I had was a laser in the left eye, the eye I had already lost. This was to clear the pieces that had broken. They gave me nothing to relax me, just put the laser straight into my eye. I was so scared.

The next operation I had was to remove the pack they put in my face; it collapsed so they had to remove it. I had a frame screwed to my face to hold it together – my head was split in two. I had steel plates put in my face to replace the bone but it turned septic so they replaced the plates with different ones. A couple of weeks after, I was flown to England, and my son accompanied me. I was taken to this place in England and as I was waiting in this house a man made me a false eye out of glass and fitted it in, but I had no socket for the eye to lie on. My son took me straight to Moorfields hospital and a doctor came to see me. He was so gentle and kind and said he would operate the next day. I needed a socket fitted. The operation took about five hours and it was a success. The doctor said the damage was very bad – he said it was the worst case he had ever seen.

The rest of my operations were on the other eye; it had fallen so the doctor took bone from my hip to hold it up. With another operation, flesh was taken from my stomach to make an eyelid – this was a success too.

Due to the accident, I lost the nerve on the right-hand

Experiencing Physical Healing

side of my face and was left with no sense of smell or taste. I suffered with whiplash for eighteen months and for four years I couldn't bend over due to dizziness. There is more, but I won't bore you with it. I shared this with you because I know what it is to suffer mentally and physically, but I really believe a happy spirit and a laughing heart is very important to keep our sanity. Sometimes we don't understand why certain people suffer more than others but I sit and think a lot and I really believe – now you don't have to believe me, but my personal opinion is that we are today what we said years ago, which is what I mentioned earlier. I believe our words rule our lives; they seem to be very powerful in the spirit world for good or bad. Sometimes, as couples, when we argue we say terrible things to hurt each other, not realising what we are doing. I believe the devil takes these words and acts upon them. He cannot touch you unless you say words that give him power to act. It's the same with God. If we speak His word, it provides faith and God can move in your life to bless you. That is His will for you. Many people have said to me many times, 'Rose, how can you still serve God after all you've been through?' Deep in my heart, all the time I knew that God wanted the best for me, so how can I not serve Him? He has been so real to me through it all. I can still live a normal life. If it wasn't for Him I would have given up long ago. Please understand, He wants the best for you and please just sit sometimes and think back: words you spoke in the past out of anger, what were the results? Sometimes we are to blame without realising what we have done.

I have shared with you, in my book, the visions I had years ago, but please understand, we can have our own

Experiencing Physical Healing

visions; they don't have to be supernatural, we can have visions of our future or of our kids' future. Our lives are better than they have been. Try not to ponder on the negative and try to see yourself in a better position than you have been in with no debt, your own house, money in the bank, all that you need in your home. Start to see it with your spiritual eye and keep on seeing it – then start to speak it. You can do it. Things are subject to change if you let them, so persevere. Life will still pass by whether you do it or not, so why not try? It's only trying to speak good things, not bad things – is that so hard? We have all been programmed to speak defeat, that's why three-quarters of the world are struggling. When Christ walked the earth He was never short of anything. Why? Because He never spoke anything but His word and good things. He was still all man as well as all God, so he was still able to fall but He persevered. Why can't we?

I really feel that writing this book, even if it only touches one person's life, will have been worth my time. My heart goes out especially to the women out there. We are classed as the weaker sex, but I believe deep inside that we are very strong and courageous and that we can change the world. God has made us with a built-in mechanism that men don't have. They have been given physical strength and power but what God has given women is far greater.

Happiness on the Faces of our Children

I THANK GOD FOR OUR husbands because sometimes we look to them for protection and security. It's a shame they don't take their position seriously because we will all answer for the role we played.

My husband and I have just come back from South Africa after having two weeks' holiday there. The reason we went was for my son's wedding. He is now thirty-three years old. We really enjoyed the wedding and our vacation. On top of it all, we got to see our daughter, the sister of the twin we lost to cancer. Well, there were many tears and hugs and a lot to catch up on. We met her in the shopping centre and she brought her two sons with her. One is fourteen and the other is six. We hadn't seen her and the one son for twelve years. It was something I needed to do before I came back.

When we were ready to fly back, we met her husband at the airport for the first time. We knew he was a black man but all those years we had to try to forgive and accept him. Thank God we did. He was very gentle and very soft. We thank God we met him. She is very happy with him, so why must we judge? God died for us all and it is by the grace and forgiveness of God that we can come through all our problems and still walk in good health and still be smiling.

It is funny, but while I have lived in Cyprus I haven't found many Christians that I feel comfortable with, and not many good churches to worship at. But God has kept

Happiness on the Faces of our Children

me strong in love and faith and I honour Him for that.

Sometimes I sit and think about the past and as a mother I only wish I could have those years back and make right all my mistakes. There is no way of rectifying them but we can improve on the future and try to be better people with God's help.

I think a lot about people in prison or on death row and it makes my heart ache and I hurt for them. I want them to understand that their sins are no bigger than ours. We have all done wrong one way or another. I want them to know that freedom comes from within ourselves and only Jesus can make you feel free when your sins are washed away, as long as we feel really sorry for what we have done in the past and know that other people can't help us because they have sinned too. So, who's without sin? Only Jesus – He was without sin and He can make us feel as clean as He feels when we come straight to Him and ask Him to help us.

I did that in 1980 and it made me feel like a new person – at last there is hope for us. We are not just left on our own with nothing to look forward to or with no hope. He is available any time of the day and He will never turn you away. He loves us so much. That world out there is cold and lonely and if we are not in the company of other people we feel so alone and lost. Sometimes we feel like that even if we are in a lot of company; it's because we miss the one who loves us and wants us with Him.

The Lord spoke to me at one time. I was in prayer and I asked him to take me back to South Africa. He asked me where my home was and I replied that it was South Africa. He said, 'No, your home is here with Me. South Africa is a country you love,' and He told me to read

Happiness on the Faces of our Children

Psalm 37 and as I read it, my mind was clear. He will give you anything you want if you love Him.

Sometimes I think back about being brought up in a house where I was abused as a teenager. I know there are many out there with the same memories, and trying to fight it on your own is not an easy task. Well, I can truly say that since I found the Lord, the damage I have inside is now bearable. You see, it can leave a terrible scar on your mind and life. You see, the scars never go away but they can fade and not be so painful. I believe there is always a reason for the mistakes we make. My heart goes out to all those who go through the same torment and sometimes, on your own, it is not easy to forgive.

I have never shared parts of what I am sharing with you in this book – not even with my own husband or family. As the victim, we feel it is our fault. I pray that if you ever read this book that you will understand that no one can heal you like Jesus.

God bless you all. I still have so much more to share in my next book.